FUN FACT FILE: ANIMAL ADAPTATIONS

20 FUN FACTS ABOUT MAMMAL ADAPTATIONS

By Kristen Rajczak

Gareth Stevens PUBLISHING

Please visit our website, www.garethstevens.com. For a free color catalog of all our high-quality books, call toll free 1-800-542-2595 or fax 1-877-542-2596.

Cataloging-in-Publication Data

Rajczak, Kristen.
20 fun facts about mammal adaptations / by Kristen Rajczak.
p. cm. — (Fun fact file: animal adaptations)
Includes index.
ISBN 978-1-4824-4450-6 (pbk.)
ISBN 978-1-4824-4394-3 (6-pack)
ISBN 978-1-4824-4432-2 (library binding)
1. Animals — Adaptation — Juvenile literature. 2. Animals — Adaptation — Miscellanea — Juvenile literature. I. Rajczak, Kristen. II. Title.
QL49.R35 2016
591.5—d23

First Edition

Published in 2017 by
Gareth Stevens Publishing
111 East 14th Street, Suite 349
New York, NY 10003

Designer: Andrea Davison-Bartolotta
Editor: Kristen Nelson

Photo credits: Cover, p. 1 Tony Campbell/Shutterstock.com; p. 5 (beaver) Simon Phipps/iStock/Thinkstock; p. 5 (macaques) Gyro Photography/amanaimagesRF/Thinkstock; p. 5 (tiger) Anup Shah/Photodisc/Thinkstock; p. 5 (duck-billed platypus) worldwildlifewonders/Shutterstock.com; p. 5 (desert fox) Nicram Sabod/Shutterstock.com; p. 5 (camel) Wolfgang Zwanzger/Shutterstock.com; p. 5 (deer) Matt Gibson/iStock/Thinkstock; p. 5 (cheetah, giraffe) Anup Shah/DigitalVision/Thinkstock; p. 5 (llamas) PavelSvoboda/Shutterstock.com; p. 5 (bat) ivkuzmin/iStock/Thinkstock; p. 5 (gorillas) Eric Gevaert/Shutterstock.com; p. 5 (whale) miblue5/iStock/Thinkstock; p. 5 (cat) banjarattanapakee/iStock/Thinkstock; p. 5 (panda) Hung Chung Chih/Shutterstock.com; p. 5 (sloth) Janossy Gergely/Shutterstock.com; p. 5 (elephants) Claudia Paulussen/Shutterstock.com; p. 5 (chipmunk) Top Photo Corporation/Top Photo Group/Thinkstock; p. 5 (bear) davidrasmus/iStock/Thinkstock; p. 5 (red panda) Ondrej Prosicky/Shutterstock.com; p. 5 (cows) Comstock/Stockbyte/Thinkstock; p. 6 Josep Pittner/Shutterstock.com; p. 7 Aleksei Verhovski/Shutterstock.com; p. 8 Jonathan Pledger/Shutterstock.com; p. 10 Bastiaan Schuit/Shutterstock.com; p. 11 (left) L Galbraith/Shutterstock.com; p. 11 (right) Vikulin/Shutterstock.com; p. 12 ironman100/iStock/Thinkstock; p. 13 wonry/Shutterstock.com; p. 14 tribal-warrior/iStock/Thinkstock; p. 15 ChrisBeverly2070/iStock/Thinkstock; p. 16 Tom linster/Shutterstock.com; p. 17 (main) Arto Hakola/Shutterstock.com; p. 17 (inset) MVPhoto/Shutterstock.com; p. 18 Wayne Lynch/Getty Images; p. 19 StevenRussellSmithPhotos/Shutterstock.com; p. 20 Jeff Foott/Getty Images; p. 21 Anthony Mercieca/Getty Images; p. 22 gnohz/Shutterstock.com; p. 23 (map) VanHart/Shutterstock.com; p. 23 (jackrabbit) Ingrid Curry/Shutterstock.com; p. 23 (vicuna) Stefano Buttafoco/Shutterstock.com; p. 23 (gazelle) Volodymyr Burdiak/Shutterstock.com; p. 23 (bilby) Susan Flashman/Shutterstock.com; p. 24 Sari Oneal/Shutterstock.com; p. 25 Popova Valeriya/Shutterstock.com; p. 26 John Macgregor/Getty Images; p. 27 James Coleman/Shutterstock.com; p. 28 Rawpixel/Shutterstock.com; p. 29 Sean Gallup/Getty Images.

Printed in the United States of America

CPSIA compliance information: Batch #CS16GS: For further information contact Gareth Stevens, New York, New York at 1-800-542-2595.

Contents

Words in the glossary appear in **bold** type the first time they are used in the text.

Marvelous Mammals

What kind of animal can be found deep in the ocean, on top of a mountain, and in a house? A mammal! Mammals are **vertebrates** and have some form of hair or fur, and most give birth to live young. There are more than 5,000 different species, or kinds, of mammals on Earth.

Mammals can live in just about every **habitat** you can think of! Over time, a mammal's body and **behaviors** change to make the animal better suited for where it lives. These changes are called adaptations.

Mammals can live in very cold and very hot weather and everything in between.

FACT 1

A mammal's heart helps it stay warm.

Unlike other kinds of animals, mammals have a heart with four chambers, or parts. The four chambers keep oxygen-rich blood coming from the **lungs** and oxygen-poor blood going to the lungs separate. Mammals are endothermic, or warm-blooded, and keeping this blood from mixing helps maintain body temperature.

Mammals like this wolf keep their body at a constant temperature regardless of the air temperature.

FACT 2

Some mammals' hair tells them about the world around them.

Whiskers are considered a kind of hair! Cats use their **sensitive** whiskers to see if they can fit into a space or to help them measure distance. Walruses use their thick whiskers to find food.

Mammal parents often teach their children how to live in their habitat, including how to find food.

FACT 3

Baby mammals are born into families.

After they're born, mammal babies are commonly raised by one or both parents. By staying with their young, mammal parents can keep their babies safe, making it more likely that they'll survive and carry on the species.

What makes a mammal?

- warm-blooded
- most give birth to live young
- single jawbone
- three middle ear bones for hearing
- four-chambered heart
- backbone
- body hair or fur
- feed milk to their young

Mammals have some features other kinds of animals don't have at all. For example, their **jaw** is connected right to their skull in one piece, instead of in two pieces like all other vertebrates.

FACT 4

There could be a dog tooth fairy!

Young dogs, like most young mammals, have a small, weak set of "baby" teeth that fall out as they grow. Stronger adult teeth then have the space to grow in. Scientists think mammals have no or small teeth at birth because their first food is milk, which isn't chewed.

Mammals' baby teeth are sometimes called "milk teeth."

FACT 5

A mammal's teeth show what they eat and how they eat it.

Carnivores, or meat eaters, have long, sharp teeth called canines near the front of their mouth to bite prey and tear at meat. Mammals that eat mostly plants don't have canines, and their teeth are flat for grinding up plants.

Beavers eat leaves, bark, and water plants.

FACT 6

A beaver's teeth never stop growing!

Beavers have rootless teeth, or teeth that will grow throughout their life. They must gnaw wood for food, but also because it wears down their teeth. If the teeth grow too long, they can cause the mammal a lot of health problems.

FACT 7

Father Dayak fruit bats may feed their babies milk.

Mammals have a special body part called a mammary gland that makes the milk their babies to drink. Both males and females have them, but they only fully **develop** for use in females—except for the Dayak fruit bat! Males make milk, too.

Scientists are still studying male Dayak fruit bats to see if the reason they make milk is to feed their babies.

FACT 8

The duck-billed platypus and echidna lay eggs.

Monotremes are part of the mammal animal group, but don't give birth to live babies like other mammals. Instead, babies develop inside eggs, like birds. There are only five monotreme species, and they're all found in New Guinea and Australia.

echidna

Keeping Warm

FACT 9

Sea otters have more than 645,000 hairs per square inch on their body.

Sea otters and some other mammals have two layers of fur that keep them warm. The underfur is soft, and the outer fur has thicker, stiffer hairs. The Pacific Ocean where otters swim is often quite cold, so they need their thick fur!

Sea otters have developed a way to open the shellfish they like to eat. They put a rock on their chest and bang the shell against it until it breaks!

Polar bears may put on so much fat that they're *too* warm in winter!

FACT 10

Polar bears may have 4.5 inches (11.4 cm) of fat on their body in winter.

Polar bears live in the Arctic. To stay warm, they have fur—it's even on the bottoms of their feet! Their coats appear white to blend in, but their skin is black to soak up the sun when it's out.

FACT 11

Stoats can change colors to hide in the snow.

Stoats, or short-tailed weasels, are commonly a dark brown color. However, when winter hits, that makes them easy to spot in the snow. Stoats have adapted by growing a white coat in the winter! This makes it harder for predators to find them.

FACT 12

An Arctic hare's ears help it stay warm.

In order to survive freezing temperatures, Arctic hares developed small ears. Shorter ears mean less body surface that needs to be warmed! Like many Arctic mammals, they have a bright white coat in the winter to blend in with the snow.

Arctic hares may also stay in groups to get warm during winter. They sometimes dig into the snow for warmth, too.

FACT 13

Deer mice don't move much during winter.

Deer mice go into torpor when it's cold. This is a state in which their body temperature is lowered and they're inactive. They also group together very closely in order to share body heat.

FACT 14

Desert mammals have a lively nightlife.

Many desert mammals keep cool in their hot, dry desert habitat by being nocturnal, or mostly active at night. Bobcats are crepuscular, meaning they're active as the sun rises and sets–not when it's at its highest in the middle of the day!

Mountain lions live in the desert, but they can also adapt to other habitats such as forests.

FACT 15

Pack rats build huge piles of desert litter up to 3 feet (0.9 m) high and 8 feet (2.4 m) long!

Desert mammals sometimes create cooler places to rest when the sun is hottest. Pack rats gather pieces of prickly pear, sticks, and stones to block the sun from the tunnels and soft nest they live in below.

FACT 16

Bighorn sheep shed in stages.

When temperatures warm up in the spring, bighorn sheep no longer need their winter coats. They shed—but not all at once. First they lose the hair on their belly and the parts of their legs in the shade of their body. Their back stays hairy to **protect** them from the hot sun!

Desert mammals around the world share adaptations such as staying in the shade, coming out only at night, and having light coloring that won't take in the sun too much.

Desert Mammals

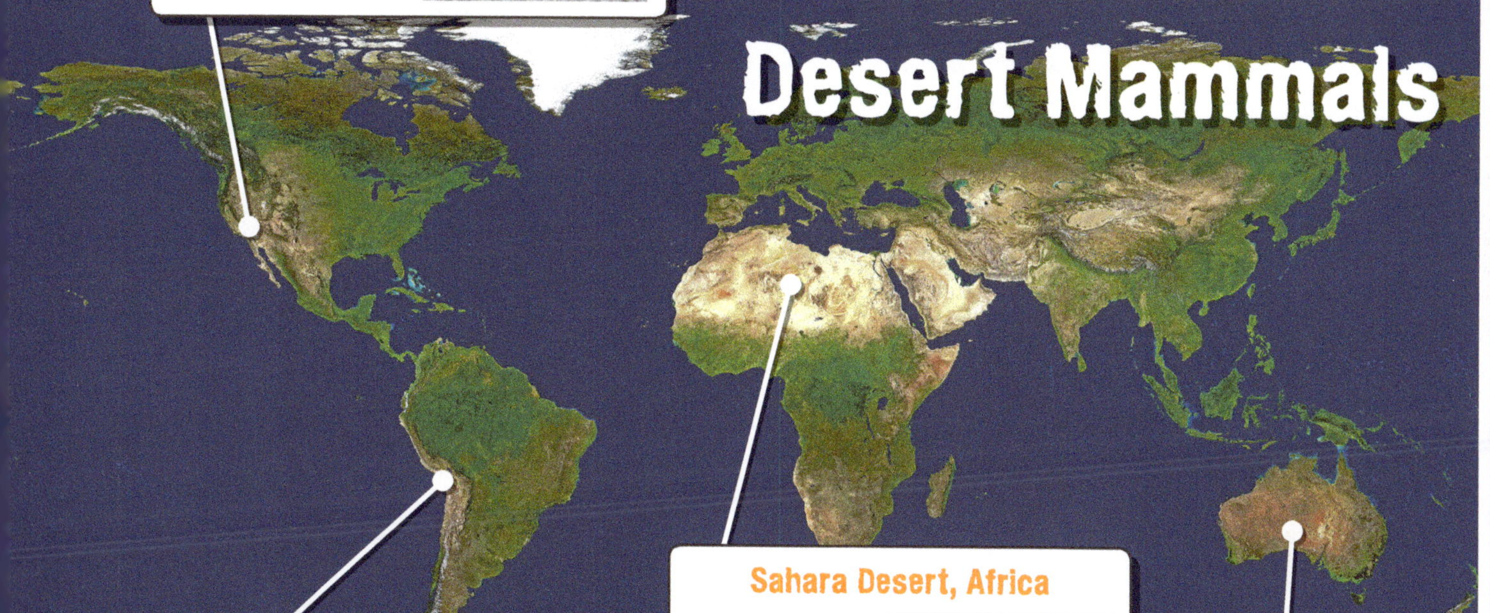

Mojave Desert, North America

- coyote
- bat
- jackrabbit
- bighorn sheep

Sahara Desert, Africa

- fennec fox
- addax antelope
- gazelle

Atacama Desert, South America

- gray fox
- vicuna
- leaf-eared mouse

Great Victoria Desert, Australia

- rock wallaby
- hopping mouse
- bilby

FACT 17

Opossums can play dead for hours.

When attacked, opossums try to fight back. If that doesn't work, they fall to the ground and stay very still. They even start to smell bad. Their predators aren't interested in eating dead animals and just leave them alone!

FACT 18

A backward charge from a crested porcupine is deadly.

This porcupine shakes its long white and black quills to make a rattling sound. If this doesn't scare a predator away, the porcupine backs into it. Short quills on its back end are **barbed** and can be pushed deep into an animal's body and cause a lot of harm.

Crested porcupine quills are large, hollow hairs. That's why they rattle when they hit each other.

FACT 19

The only North American mammal with a poisonous bite weighs less than an ounce!

Northern short-tailed shrews' venom, or poison, is used on their prey. They also give off musk, or a scent, that both smells and tastes bad to the weasels and foxes that may try to eat them.

The northern short-tailed shrew can be found in parts of Canada and as far south as Nebraska and Georgia. They don't often bite people, but may if they're picked up.

FACT 20

Getting sprayed directly by a skunk can cause blindness for a time.

Skunks, weasels, and ferrets can all spray musk that smells terrible! They're just trying to keep predators away. Skunk musk is perhaps the most powerful. Their eyesight, on the other hand, isn't good at all, so they need a good **defense**!

The Best-Known Mammal

A mammal you're very familiar with also has a number of adaptations—humans! Like other mammals, people develop adaptations depending on where they live. For example, people who live on the Tibetan **plateau** have adapted to living at high **altitudes** by breathing faster than those who live at sea level!

Adaptations are all a part of evolution, or the changes that occur in animals over time. Modern mammals, including people, are all products of evolution. Because we've adapted, we've survived!

Anthropology, or the study of humans, includes a look at climatic adaptations. These are the body and behavior developments that have occurred in response to people's surroundings.

Glossary

altitude: height above sea level

barbed: having a barb, or a sharp point that bends backward and isn't easy to remove

behavior: the way an animal acts

defense: a way of guarding against an enemy

develop: to grow and change over time

habitat: the natural place where an animal or plant lives

jaw: the bottom bone of the mouth in which teeth are fixed

lung: a part of an animal that takes in air when it breathes

plateau: a large area of land with raised sides and a level top

protect: to keep safe

sensitive: able to sense or feel changes in surroundings

vertebrate: an animal with a backbone

For More Information

Books

Herrington, Lisa M. *Amazing Mammals.* New York, NY: Children's Press, 2016.

Jackson, Tom. *Animal.* New York, NY: DK Publishing, 2012.

Martin, Isabel. *Mammals: A Question and Answer Book.* North Mankato, MN: Capstone Press, 2015.

Websites

Animals: Facts, Pictures, and Videos
kids.nationalgeographic.com/animals/
Discover many animals and all their cool features.

Top 10 Animal Adaptations
www.animalplanet.com/wild-animals/animal-adaptations/
Read about some very cool animal adaptations.

Index